The Inner Consciousness

I0190996

How to Awaken and Direct It

By
SWAMI PRAKASHANANDA

Revised and Edited by

Dennis Logan

[2020]

THE INNER CONSCIOUSNESS

How to Awaken and Direct It

In theoretical as well as applied psychology no term is more misleading, or confusing than the term consciousness. We use the term often in our conversation; we come across it in our study; but when we are asked to define it properly, to explain its significance, its meaning, or the idea for which that word stands, we are unable to do so. And that is because there are so many varied ideas concerning consciousness. There are so many aspects of consciousness, there are so many states of consciousness that we get mixed up—that is, we confuse one with the other. So we must know thoroughly the true significance of the term. Then we can make such distinctions as inner consciousness and outer consciousness.

What is truly meant by consciousness, or what is the principle back of that term? There are many ideas which cannot be expressed properly for lack of words, or lack of terms. The word consciousness is really derived from the Latin root **Scio**, to know, and **con**, together; so the word consciousness from the derivative meaning would signify: to know together. We use the term generally in the sense of being conscious of a fact. That is, consciousness means knowing an object, as it were; knowing something. But the word consciousness really indicates two things—subject and object. It implies the duality of existence. There is one who is the knower, the subject, the ego, the perceiver. I know it; I am conscious of it; I perceive it; I think about it. Therefore there is always the subject, the ego—I—as the background of any form of consciousness.

Then there must be something to be conscious of, something which we perceive, something which we know, something which we understand, and that something is the object. So, "knowing together" means we know the subject and object together—that is, they both exist; one cannot exist without the other. So wherever there is a subject, there is also an object. That means that wherever there is a thinker, there must be something to think about; otherwise there is no meaning back of the term "thinker".

Whenever we use the term "perceiver", we must know that there is something to be perceived. The same is true of consciousness. Whenever we use the term "consciousness", we must know it includes both—the one who is conscious of something, and something of which that one is conscious. Therefore the word "consciousness" implies duality.

There is another meaning back of "consciousness" which we often fail to understand, or about which we do not stop to think deeply. That is why we miss it. Consciousness not only implies the idea of becoming conscious of a thing, or the state of being conscious of something, but there is also the idea of identification back of it.

What is the meaning of identification? By identification we mean a state in which we become almost one with a thing. When we become one with a thing we become conscious of it. Of course ordinarily we may not be wholly identified with it, but the word consciousness indicates that, and judging our modes of thought, or observing the practical phases of our life, we shall see that there is identification.

Take for instance, the word "body-consciousness". What does it mean? It means that not only are we conscious of the body, but we are also identified with it. I cannot separate myself from the body; I am almost one with it. I have become mixed up, as it were, with the body and its conditions. There the subject or ego is hidden; only the object of consciousness, the object of perception is there. So that is another meaning of consciousness.

The deepest and purest meaning of consciousness is this: the absolute consciousness. There is the Sanskrit word "chit". You will come across that word in the study of the Upanishads, in the Vedas, in the Gita, and in many such books. You will find not only ancient sages, but the sages of modern times have been using the term "Sat-chit-ananda", meaning the Divine Spirit. Sat-chit-ananda—what is its meaning? It means absolute existence, absolute consciousness, absolute bliss. These three are not the qualities of the Divine Spirit, but they are the essence—one with it. So chit is the word of pure consciousness. In the understanding of pure consciousness, we have to eliminate the duality of existence, the duality of subject and object. It stands alone; it is that of which the subject and object are lower manifestations, or expressions. It is that which makes everything possible, which gives life and soul to the subject and object, as it were. So that is pure consciousness, the basic, the fundamental, the principle back of everything that is indicated by pure consciousness.

There is a beautiful Sanskrit verse which expresses this idea.

"Na Tatra Suryo bhati na chandra tarakam
Nema Vidyuto bhanti Kutoyam agni
Tameva bhantam anubhati sarvam
Tasya bhasha Sarvamidam bibhati"
(Kathopanishad, Chap. V. 15).

In describing the pure, the basic, fundamental principle of life and creation—the pure light, the self-effulgent, self-caused Divine Intelligence—Vedic sages sang in this way: "There the sun does not shine, nor the moon, nor the lightning, what to speak of the mortal fire. That shining, everything shines; by its light everything is illumined",—by its essence everything becomes full of consciousness.

There is another Sanskrit word which expresses the same idea, Kaivalyam, the state of being alone; that which is self-caused; that which is not dependent on anything; that which is freedom itself; which is above everything. Do you see? There all differentiation vanishes— differentiation of subject and object, I and thou. All these ideas are merged, as it were, in that absolute consciousness. So the pure consciousness is that.

However, when we apply the term consciousness in our daily lives, in its varied relation to various channels of existence, in our varied experiences, in different states and conditions, we have to understand it from a dualistic standpoint, and we also have to study other phases of consciousness, such as inner consciousness and outer consciousness, soul-consciousness and body consciousness. All these terms we bring in to explain the different details, or the different stages of development, or the different stages of experience through which we have to pass.

In order to be able to understand the inner consciousness, we must know it in its relation to the outer consciousness. The light can be understood only in its relation to darkness. Praise can be understood only in its relation to blame. Joy can be understood only in its relation to suffering or pain. One who is not really hungry cannot really appreciate the value of food. So, many ideas exist only relatively. It is the same with the inner and outer consciousness. We must understand both—then both become clear. What is meant then by outer consciousness? Outer consciousness means consciousness in which we are cognizant of external things—gross forms, gross objects, sense objects. Now, every moment of our lives, the senses bring in these impressions. The senses come in touch with the external objects of nature, gross things, gross objects, objects of vision, objects of touch, objects of taste. All these objects of perception exist in gross form, and there is the impression within ourselves, or there are impressions of varied sorts. That is outer consciousness—

consciousness of the outer-world, the objective world.

I am not going to enter here into a detailed exposition of what is called idealism, or realism. But outer consciousness must mean this to us: there is the idea of objective perception, and there is the objective world. We know that there is external nature, and all the time we are impressed with this idea. So when we cannot extricate ourselves from the realm and domain of forms and objects, when we cannot rise above the sense perceptions—the gross sense perceptions—when we cannot divest our minds of these externalities, as it were, then you will understand this state to be the outer consciousness.

Coming nearer the practical idea—there is the body-consciousness. As I stated previously, that means that we are conscious of the body, the body in all its phases, in all its senses, and in all its aspects.

Then there is a consciousness within ourselves. You may say that only through mind can we understand this, only through thought processes can we get knowledge of external nature. That is true, but in order to explain the inner consciousness properly, I have to bring in this idea of the outer consciousness where all these things exist; where there are nothing but external things, nothing but sense impressions, nothing but outer objects and their impressions.

What is meant by inner consciousness? Inner consciousness means: consciousness of inner forces, consciousness of inner perceptions, consciousness of what is called soul energy, consciousness of the Divine in the soul. That is a consciousness of something distinct and separate from the sense impressions, from bodily conditions, from external gross objects, from external perceptions.

Now this question may arise in your mind: Why should we try to awaken our inner consciousness? What benefit do we gain by it? We always ask that question. What are we going to gain by it? Why should we try to arouse the inner consciousness, if the outer consciousness is as explained? What harm is there in living in the outer consciousness only? Our life means that, our life means the varied duties of life—the varied responsibilities. Our life means its relation to our fellow-beings, to the world, to so many material things, to so many objects, to so many phases of external life. Our life means all this—and what is the harm in living in that state of consciousness? Why should we try to awaken our inner consciousness? Is there any necessity for it? Is it absolutely necessary—is it indispensably necessary to enter that life? Yes, it is absolutely necessary for persons in all walks of life. Why? Because while living in the outer consciousness we are not really contented. We always complain, either openly or mentally. Something is always lacking in our life. Just ask yourself this question: Are we really happy? It is not that we have to give up our external life, our material life. It is not that we have to eliminate all these things completely from our life. No. But we have to know where we stand, and we have to understand the purpose and the meaning of our external life, or outer consciousness. We must know why we have to go through life's duties. We must know why we have to perform so many activities. What is the purpose? What is the idea back of it? Why are those condemned who neglect their duties, who shirk their responsibilities, who do not try to perform their functions, their duties properly? The idea is this: First of all, we are ignorant of the meaning and purpose of life. We cannot explain definitely the reason for all these activities. We do not know why we live in the midst of sense perceptions. Why are we experiencing these things? We have certain desires, we have certain tendencies, certain emotions, certain passions. We are regulated by them; we are carried away by them against our will. We are, as it were, enslaved by certain things, and we go on, not knowing whence we have come or whither we are going, or what is the mission of our life. That is why the question was asked in ancient times by the Vedic sages:

"What is that, knowing which, everything else will be known?" What is that fountainhead, knowing which, we shall understand the meaning and purpose of life— knowing which, everything would be explained? Everything appears to be detached, purposeless, meaningless. What is that, knowing which, everything would be illumined? That is the question. That is the desire, in reality, in every human heart. We may not be able to explain it; we may not know it properly at times; but it is there, and only the sages have put the question definitely. That is why we must try to get into that realm of pure consciousness, as I explained. There are different grades of inner consciousness. The deeper we search, the more we understand, the more will that pure consciousness be unfolded which alone holds the key. To illuminate, to unfold, to explain everything in our life, we must come to that.

There is another reason why we must try to go beyond the outer and enter into the inner consciousness, and that is this: There is always reaction in our life—that is, when we live in the external consciousness, there is always reaction. Suffering is caused by reaction. Our miseries, our pains, our complaints, our doubts, our troubles, our disillusionments, our despair, have always been caused by the outer consciousness. For instance, when we live in the midst of sense perceptions we want to possess certain objects which we have perceived, impressions of which have been gathered through the senses. First of all, the senses come in touch with external things.

It may be a little food, a little form; it may be a little object; but it is there. That impression gets hold of us, and what do we want to do? We want to get that object; we want to possess it; we want to own it. When we cannot own it, there is suffering, there is heart-burning.

Suppose I love some object. I try my best to possess it. I cannot do it. Something stands in the way and takes it away from me—snatches it away. There is suffering. There is misery. In this way we are constantly becoming dependent on external things. These outer things, these external things, these objects of the senses get hold of us. They enter our lives and completely hold sway over us, and we are carried away by them. Then we are thrown back, as it were, into ourselves; because nature's laws work relentlessly—and there are changes—there are separations.

You may say such ideas bring gloominess, pessimism into our lives. What difference does it make if we become a little gloomy, or if we become pessimistic? What has your optimism given us? What do the passing joys bring us? They bring us nothing but reaction. So-called optimism does not land us anywhere. It rather leads us into complex situations and conditions. Rather we should hail with joy that sort of pessimism, true pessimism, which brings us face to face with the truth, which enables us to see things in their true color. Yes, we must face things boldly. It is not simply by patchwork that we gain in life, it is only by bold search and uncompromising investigation. It is by going to the root and the bottom of things that we gain—truly gain—

and accomplish something which is worth achieving. So we must not be afraid of analyzing things in a deeper way. You see around you nature's changes and separations. You love a person. That person dies, or is taken away to other lands. You are miserable and prostrated with grief. Again, you have possessed certain things and you lose them— you lose a fortune in a few days, or in a few weeks, or in a few months. You are overcome with sorrow. That is life, and that is what is meant by outer consciousness. It is not that you must not have possessions; it is not that you must not have good homes; it is not that you must not love others. But do it knowingly; do it not as a slave, but as a master; not as a dependent worm, but as the witness you should approach these things.

Many things there are which must be taken into our lives necessarily. Unhappily we delude ourselves; we forget ourselves; we lose our heads; we lose our judgment; and we are carried away by the currents of life, not knowing whither we are going. When we are caught up in the whirl of conditions, when we are lost in the labyrinthian maze of circumstances, then we wake up for a while. Again we forget. So that is the outer consciousness, which has separations everywhere. You cannot depend upon anything. As soon as you depend upon anything—lean on anything—it is taken away from you, and what is to be done? That is why we must try to search for something which is more internal, which is not so changeable, on whom, or on which you can depend to a greater extent, because everything is relative until we get to the Absolute. We must
find something which is better,

which is greater. And that is our search—that should be our search. So, while living a life of outer consciousness you will analyze and you will see how all your complex conditions regarding which you complain, all the entanglements which we notice in different lives, all the confusion and friction which we see at home or abroad, all the heart-burnings, disillusionment and suffering which we notice amongst individuals—all these can be traced to that outer consciousness, that slavery, that dependence upon the material things of life. That is why we have to open up our inner consciousness. That is why we want to know if there is anything beyond the veil of the senses. That is why we must know whether there is anything back of this changeable condition of the senses and this changeable condition of the body.

Now, you may ask the question, how do we know that there is such a thing as soul-energy, or that there are inner forces? How do we know? We know as we know everything in life. We have to follow the same methods. How do you know the different details of a machine? You study that machine. You follow three processes—that is, three steps you must take in everything. First of all, you get hold of a book, or you go to a person who knows about the machine and you ask him questions. You look over different descriptions of the details of the machine, then you think for yourself; you judge for yourself. You revolve all these details within your mind. You analyze, and gradually you begin to handle the machine yourself—practical experience you must acquire.

For instance, if you want to know about electricity, what do you do? You get hold of a book on the subject of electricity. Then you go to a professor and receive instruction. Then you go to the laboratory and handle different machines and study them.

Suppose you want to learn music, you follow the same process. And it is the same with this subject of the inner consciousness. First of all, you have to study; you must read books, or you must consult some persons who know. Would you believe blindly? Would you accept blindly that which they tell you? No. In no study must we accept anything blindly. Blind belief does not lead us anywhere. We must search thoroughly without any fear. Truth can stand all the tests of analysis, all the tests of observation. And if it is not truth, it cannot stand the test.

So always keep the reasoning faculty, or power of analysis sharpened, ready to observe, ready to understand, ready to reason out. At every point you must reason. And the more is this true with regard to the study of these inner things. Why? Because there are so many dangers and difficulties in studying these inner things. Many promising lives have been failures owing to a lack of proper understanding, owing to ignorance, owing to indiscriminate search or indiscriminate investigation. You cannot be too cautious—you cannot be too careful in studying these things.

These, then, are the steps you have to take. First, study and go to a person who has studied these things and who knows these things. In every book you will notice you are asked to go to a teacher. As you need a teacher in different fields of knowledge, so you need a teacher in this field too, and the more so because the objects which you are going to learn, the principles which you are going to master, are so subtle. Machines you can handle properly, because they are external things. You can grasp them. You can see them. But in studying this subject you have to study that which is very subtle, which is very fine. That is why you need more care. You need the help, you need the guidance of someone who is an expert teacher. And then you analyze yourself and reason—always reason. But do not bring that sort of skepticism into your life which is dangerous, which, as it were, clogs up all the channels of experience, which covers, or shuts up, all the avenues of knowledge, which makes one give up the search without proper study and investigation. Do not become skeptical in that way.

Many have a tendency to become skeptical and give up the search. We have no honest right to demand any knowledge unless we have studied properly, or investigated closely. So open your mind, your heart, your soul to conviction. At the same time, do not take anything for granted, but be ready to learn. Always be receptive, always be responsive. Then we have to apply certain direct means; we have to follow certain practical methods in order to accomplish our purpose.

Now, of all the different methods which are handed down to us from the great sages and masters, one method is important, and that is concentration. Why is concentration upheld as a great method? Can we not awaken the inner consciousness by prayer, by worship, by devotion, by Divine love, and in many other ways? Certainly, we can. But in the path of concentration we can rise step by step—it is the most scientific method. Of course every path can be made scientific we may say, or every path can be followed step by step. True. But we can combine certain methods. Take, for instance, devotion. Devotion is a great thing. The love for an ideal, we need; it is important; in this country it is necessary. But if we allow ourselves to be carried away by heightened emotions, or by wrought-up feelings, we may develop fanaticism. There have been instances in which devotion, love, Divine love—when not combined with proper concentration, or proper analysis—have landed persons in the realm of emotionalism, or sentimentality, or fanaticism. They are led into the realm of bigotry and narrowness and carried away by these things. So try to balance devotion, with proper reasoning and it will be a great, helpful method. True prayer can open up our inner communion and help us to unfold. Pure self-analysis is another method. But concentration has been found to be very helpful for many, many people—for the majority of people—if it can be followed under the guidance of proper teachers and if it can be followed methodically. But some might say that there is danger in concentration. There is no danger in concentration. Consciously or unconsciously we apply it in every field of knowledge. Without concentration what can you do? As Emerson said, "The one prudence in life is concentration; the one evil is dissipation." In war, in politics, in business, in trade, in the management of all commercial and social affairs, concentration is the secret of success.

And what is meant by concentration? Concentration

includes two things. One is gathering up scattered energies; another is focusing these scattered energies of mind.

As I explained, outer consciousness means this: We are dependent on the senses and outward things. That is, when we try to think of inner things, we are held back by our dependence on things external. We are all the time living in these external impressions, and cannot enter into the inner realm of understanding.

And how does concentration help us? Concentration helps us to withdraw our scattered minds from different directions. The mind has been scattered. It wanders among various objects, which are impressions in our minds. The mind has been divided, and thus mental energy is dissipated. Very little energy is left for the accomplishment of the real ideals in life. But gradually we learn by concentration how to withdraw the scattered forces of the mind and how to focus them upon the chosen ideal.

There are many details, but I am only mentioning the most important points.

When, through proper training and daily practice, one is able to learn how to gather up the wandering mind, and withdraw these different powers of the mind from different sources and focus them on one thing, then so much energy has been combined, as it were, and we can accomplish something. Otherwise, so much of our energy has been dissipated.

Regarding the difficulties and dangers of concentration, let me mention that there are difficulties in all paths, in all fields of knowledge. Nothing worth achieving has been accomplished without a little difficulty, without a little sacrifice, without a little sincere and earnest effort. You know, curiosity-seekers never reach anything in life. Those who are sincere and earnest searchers and seekers have gradually unfolded themselves and reached the higher realms of understanding. So there is no real danger in concentration. We must start with that idea, and not be hasty. Many of us try to take things like a pill. We take a pill, and it must accomplish its results. Concentration is not a pill—and we do not know what accumulated experiences and impressions are at our backs. Through different lives and through the present life we have been gathering up so many things. We are performing so many karmas, as we say, and we have to eliminate so many things in our lives. Through proper effort we shall remove many obstacles, many difficulties, and our task will become easier and easier.

Now, the Yogis, in figurative language call this opening up of the inner consciousness the awakening of the Kundalini. You will see—if you analyze your life—that there are a few things which are constantly holding your attention. The mind, as it were, is drawn into certain realms. As I explained in the beginning, sense perceptions are in different forms and include many things—our eating, our drinking, all sorts of habits and many other things. Thus the best of our energies are swallowed up, as it were, by these things. The Yogis claim that the nerve centers—the lower nerve centers—have absorbed these energies and the energies are chained there, or enslaved there, and you have to release them. There are two sides, the physiological and mental. Physiologically, when we begin to practice concentration, this energy is gradually released from the lower centers. It is called the awakening of Kundalini—coiled-up energy—energy in latent form or enslaved form. Simultaneously our mind is released from its impressions and begins to work in a higher realm.

Time will not permit me to enter into the details of this subject, but I just want to touch upon some important points, so that you will think and study and investigate more.

A few points I must try to impress upon your mind. I must repeat that first of all these things should be studied under the guidance of proper teachers, and secondly, that you need not believe anything blindly. I want to impress this upon your mind because these things are established facts and those who have experienced them know these things. They are not the results of mere speculation, or mere imagination, because those teachers who would try to teach you will tell you from the beginning that you have to eliminate all the ideas of imagination. You must give up imagining things. Many of us have a tendency to imagine too much, constantly seeing visions and other things. You must eliminate those notions from the beginning, and must try to live in realities, in facts and true experiences. So you must not accept anything credulously, but try to study and investigate for yourself.

The Yogis declare that there is a hollow canal in the spinal column, and that the base of the spinal column, in the majority of persons, is closed. When these energies are released, they must find a passage and they must be allowed to go through this canal, and as this released energy rises into higher and higher centers, we enter into inner and inner stages of illumination. And when that energy reaches the brain—the highest center, the pineal gland—there the illumination becomes absolute; that is, we reach that pure state of consciousness of which I have spoken.

You will find as you progress that there are physiological experiences and mental experiences. As we have physiological experiences we shall see that the whole nervous system is changing. Our bodies are full of vibrating currents. Our whole life is full of vibrating currents, and we must know how to direct them, how to adjust them. And that is why I said the teachers would ask you to give up that idea of imagining things. We imagine and speculate too much. We must not accept anything unless it is realized, and that is why the student must be properly directed.

And why is it necessary that the student should be directed? Because of ignorance of the subtle forces involved. As these physiological experiences go on, layer after layer of the mind is opened up, but you must let these experiences alone. You must not identify yourself with them. Do you not see that in order to eliminate these external conditions and enter into the inner realms of consciousness, we have to rise above the body consciousness? Therefore, if we identify ourselves with these vibrations, or any kind of physiological experiences, we are going against what we are trying to accomplish. We would be inconsistent. So put the chemicals together and let the crystallization take care of itself. Gradually the latent energy awakens, and the energy working in the life is concentrated. Gradually you will see a new vista of knowledge and wisdom opening before you. A new land, a new realm of experience is coming to you, and that needs the master mind. Instead of allowing ourselves to become enslaved again by these conditions, we must rise above them as the master. We must become the director. Instead of allowing the mind to take the reins, we must take the reins in our own hands. You, as part of the Divine Spirit, have that mastery and power. You have that strength within you, and you are going to be the director. And so you have to tell the mind and the senses and the little things in your life that you are the master. They must know who is the master, and who is going to direct the situation. In this way we have to direct properly, knowing the ideal thoroughly, knowing where we are going, what we are trying to accomplish, eliminating all the selfish ideals, eliminating all the obstacles and difficulties as much as possible.

Yes, there are obstacles; there are difficulties, and we are frightened by them. But you must remember these difficulties and obstacles can be overcome. They come to test our strength, and we overcome them, we unfold our latent and dormant powers. So never give way. Never give up after you accept a method. Be not hasty in adopting a method, but once you have taken it up, follow it with the utmost pertinacity. Follow it with that sincerity and earnestness of purpose necessary for accomplishment in all walks of life and in all fields of achievement. And then go on, day after day, practicing it, following it with un-ending patience and perseverance.

Gradually a time will come when you will see that there is a realm, or there are different realms of inner consciousness which are being unfolded to you. By degrees you will come to that state of Divine illumination which will make you really blessed. The blessedness of that state cannot be described—it must be felt—it must be experienced.

I will conclude this topic with the admonition that we must be absolutely sincere, and we must not apply these things in any other way than for spiritual unfoldment. There is the danger. We have a tendency to apply them in different realms—lower states—and for selfish purposes. We must avoid that. To many, you must remember, it may be a life task. For many, it may take several lives. Some may accomplish it in a few years. To others, again—persons of sincerity and steadfastness—it may come quickly. But whatever time it takes, we must be determined and we must start with this idea, that even before passing away from this life, we will reach a very high state of consciousness, and we will unfold that Divine, cosmic, universal, absolute consciousness, which alone can make us really happy and blessed.

www.ingramcontent.com/pod-product-compliance
Lightning Source LLC
Chambersburg PA
CBHW071749020426
42331CB00008B/2237